# The Fruit of the Spirit

## And Martial Arts

### Written by Eric Stieg

### Edited by Joyce Dujardin

For information about first time authors, contact Fifth Estate, Post Office Box 116, Blountsville, AL 35031.

First Edition

Edited by Joyce A. Dujardin
Cover Designed by An Quigley

Printed on acid-free paper

Library of Congress Control No: 2005921757

ISBN: 0-9760992-5-X

Fifth Estate, 2005

# Table of Contents

# Acknowledgements

This book would never have come to fruition if God hadn't placed me in an environment where so many people had been asking for a Christian martial arts ministry. Without His leadership, provision of experiences in my life, or relentless focus, this book would have remained an idea indefinitely.

This book is undoubtedly the culmination of many people's wisdom, ideas, and understanding. Specifically, how closely knit a personal walk with Christ can become through the study of Christian based martial arts. Most notable, is my right hand man through the development of this book, Mr. John Schroeder, whose kindred spirit and "lead by example" mentality epitomizes the servant leadership qualities found in a Christian martial artist. Thank you for your consistency, dedication, and humbleness. Without you, this ministry and the words in this book would never have reached outside of our local program.

To my publicist, Joyce Dujardin, who consistently followed up with me to make sure I would finish this book. Her enthusiasm and interest for this project was contagious! Thank you for continually providing words of encouragement, and at times the proverbial "get with it!"

Mr. Eric Bauer, who instructed me in Tae Kwon Do back in the early 1990's and was pivotal in helping me realize that martial arts would be part of my life until the good Lord calls me home.  Eric, I would never have continued to this point if it hadn't been for your enthusiasm for the arts, your long hours of studying Korean terminology back in the dorm room, and your pursuit of helping others attain their martial art goals. Your example some 15 years ago helped me realize I too could help others reach their martial arts goals.

What book could be completed without the support of family? To my parents back home who told me I could succeed in anything if I set my mind to it, I thank you.  You laid the foundation for me and my family by providing a God-filled home.  You taught me I could achieve and be an example to others.

I must also thank my wonderful children, Grayson and Gabrielle, who are a constant inspiration and reminder to stay healthy and be active so I may enjoy them for many years to come.  I enjoy every day with you both jumping into my arms after a long day at work.  You encompass what this book strives to discover.

Lastly, to my wife, you've given me an opportunity to help others and share God's word in a unique and compelling way. The long nights waiting for me to come home have paid off. You are a wonderful example of a Christian woman. Your confidence in me and unwavering unconditional love you provide is truly an undeserving gift. I thank God every morn, for He has blessed me with you in my life!

# Introduction

This book came about by accident.  After a few years of developing lesson plans for the local church martial arts program, it dawned on me this information needed to be shared with others outside the area.  Sometimes God's plans aren't made apparent until much later in our journey with Him.  That certainly is the case with this book.  Today, we have multiple schools across the country requesting information, sending success stories and asking for more lessons.  I only ask that you give me time.

The Fruit of the Spirit and Martial Arts is a culmination of Biblical versus and principles found throughout the Old and New Testaments.  Specifically, the book creates a framework for how these principles relate to a personal walk with Christ while learning martial arts and self defense.  Christian character attributes, found in Galatians 5:22, indicate love, joy, peace, patience, kindness, goodness, faithfulness, gentleness, and self-control as the Fruit of the Spirit.  The book has been developed as a teaching and learning tool within the martial arts training hall.  My hope is you will, as instructors and students, use the lessons found throughout this book as a starting point to understanding how the study and practice of martial arts can bring you closer to Christ.

In the secular world, a martial arts program may focus solely on fighting, incapacitation or street brutality tactics to ensure ones peace of mind or survival. If you look at today's youth; aggression, physical confrontation and boastfulness are praised as the characteristics one should strive for to be successful. I believe this mentality festers a belief that power over gentleness, force over self-control, immediacy over patience are the only ways to solve conflict. This book helps identify another way to solving problems. By focusing on Christ as our example, believing in oneself, and understanding the true definition of meekness, we can overcome problems in a peaceful, long term and non-confrontational manner.

It's often been said in the martial arts community, if you find yourself in a confrontation, you have already lost. This book lays the groundwork for understanding the Fruit of the Spirit should help in guiding our decisions. In <u>Tao of Jeet Kune Do</u>, Bruce Lee said, "Before I studied the art, a punch to me was just a punch, a kick was just a kick. After I'd studied the art, a punch was no longer a punch, a kick no longer a kick. Now that I understand the art, a punch is just a punch, a kick is just a kick." This journey of understanding, of applying knowledge to physical and mental skills, is the basis for the lessons in this book. I believe you will understand why a physical confrontation is always the lesser means to an end result.

My hope is you will finish this book and have a more thorough understanding how each of us goes through this journey of becoming a better person through Christ's help. If you read this book, and apply the principles to your personal life and your martial arts discipline, you will find yourself more engaged in disciplining your mind and spirit as opposed to just disciplining your body through punches and kicks. Your concentration and focus in and outside the training hall will be heightened, your acceptance of others, discernment, humility, and gentleness will increase as you begin to understand the true definition of meekness, success, and Christ's undying love for His children. You will reach your full potential by understanding, nurturing, and growing in the Fruit of the Spirit and martial arts.

# How to Read This Book

The book is intended as a training hall tool so instructors and students can openly discuss the lessons during what we call "sharing time." You'll notice the chapters are focused on three main categories; *Christian Character Attributes & Character Development, Disciplining your Mind and Body,* and *Being a Person of Action.* These chapters include specific scripture references and how they relate to training in the martial arts.

While perusing the lessons, you'll notice most begin with a scripture verse. A "what does this mean to me" or "context" section follows, with examples of how the opening scriptures relate to martial arts training, or events in today's world. Share stories from your own life to help students learn about you as the instructor! Unless otherwise noted, all scripture versus are quoted from *The Inspirational Study Bible, New King James Version,* by Word Bibles.

At the very end of each lesson, you'll notice a short statement which is intended to summarize the lesson. If you read only one portion of a lesson, I encourage you to read this bolded summary line. We've seen the proverbial "light go on" when the summary statement is discussed. I would like to further encourage you to use your own training and real-life examples to further strengthen the discussion, but also the relationship you have with your students. There's nothing like a black belt instructor sharing a little bit of his or her own experience and heart with the students!

Adding your own personal touch to the lessons will only increase the respect others have for you. Seeing you as an example of someone who's not afraid to share will help your student's realize they can do the same. A real sense of security will permeate your training hall as students come to realize they are not the only one with difficulties, obstacles and challenges in their life. You, as the instructor, set the example by appreciating student's personal experiences. This, in turn, helps them realize they are valued and loved, which will go a long way to building their self-esteem and confidence. When these building blocks are used, you will become the example Christ calls us to be.

After each lesson, you'll notice discussion questions which relate to the corresponding lesson. The questions were developed with younger students in mind. Depending on the age and skill level of the students in your class, you may want to use these questions as a starting point for more in-depth topics. I encourage you to highlight, underscore, and make notes throughout the book!

After the discussion questions, you will find a short prayer. It is included for two reasons; praying with others will help eliminate barriers or difficulties in your class. Who can pray to the all knowing God and have malice in their heart? Praying with others builds a common bond. Secondly, by praying with your students, they see you as an example of something they aspire to! As an example, my 4 year old son often reminds the family to hold hands around the dinner table and pray. He does this because we have been his example. He knows it is the right thing to do. On the occasion we "forget" to pray, he politely reminds us we need to remember God. Do this in your training hall, and your students will come to expect it. What a terrific way to encourage them to pray at home and become prayer warriors!

# ~ **Chapter 1** ~

# **The Fruit of the Spirit and Martial Arts**

I am often asked by students why the Fruit of the Spirit isn't known as the "Fruits" of the Spirit. Based upon our English language, you would think these gifts, which are numerous and bountiful, would be considered plural. The Bible defines the Fruit of the Spirit as, "love, joy, peace, patience, kindness, goodness, faithfulness, gentleness and self-control, against such things there is no law."

While reading this book, it is important to realize the "Fruit" the Bible speaks of comes from a single source – the Holy Spirit. The giver of these gifts provides the Fruit to each person in order to glorify God and to help each other. My belief is the singular word "Fruit" is used because it is a gift not only provided by "one" Holy Spirit, but the gift is given to glorify our "one" creator and heavenly Father. Therefore, the Fruit of the Spirit is given freely to each person that walks in communion with our heavenly Father, but also those who use their gift to bear "fruit" in others lives, by being an example of love, joy, peace, etc., When we surround ourselves with people of like mentality, we enrich our lives and those around us. We become the recipients of others bearing fruit and sharing in the wealth of gifts the Holy Spirit provides.

The Fruit of the Spirit describes a person who walks in a personal relationship with Christ. Each person, through Christ, has a different amount of each fruit, and each fruit has a different shape or perspective in each person – but all the fruit will show in each Christian as he or she progresses in their walk with Christ. Martial arts can be the conduit for allowing that personal walk with Christ to strengthen and enhance those gifts.

If you review the cover of this book, you will notice each Fruit of the Spirit surrounds an image. The image represents an open Bible, from which our understanding and knowledge of God can grow. The two vines represent our Father in heaven, who continually replenishes us and provides meaning to our life. By studying God's word, He unveils his Love for us. Through Christ's death on the cross, we are pruned and replenished by God to do His will. Being reborn through His Spirit, we can be an example to this world. The example we must be is that of the Fruit of the Spirit!

The martial arts are based upon the same foundation. In a secular training hall, the Fruit of the Spirit (referred to as

FOTS) may appear as; courtesy, integrity, perseverance, self-control and indomitable spirit. There is a major disparity between a Christian martial artist's view of these attributes and the view shared in the secular world. Unless you walk in a personal relationship with Christ, you cannot exemplify the FOTS, or the equivalent secular definition, to their fullest potential.

As an example, think of the word joy. To the world, joy may mean having a birthday, getting a new car, buying a new house, or getting married. Joy to a Christian takes on an entirely different meaning. The Bible calls us to have joy, not because of "happenings" like those listed above, but because we know Christ is there for us, will carry us through difficult times, and bring us to new heights. Most importantly, we can have joy because of the knowledge that Christ died for us and has gone to prepare a great place for His children.

Yes, a martial artist in the secular world can have joy! One of the greatest joys of my life and others I trained with was obtaining a first degree black belt in various arts. A secular martial artist defines courtesy, integrity, perseverance and self-control as *outward actions that can be controlled through one's internal will power.* In the secular world, the belief that, "I can control this situation, or have self-control and perseverance through this test because I am prepared, I am focused, I am the master of my domain," is unnerving and false. This self-belief, that a person's individual power, their own focus, and their internal strength are sufficient to succeed, is a fallacy.

Conversely, the Christian martial artist realizes these are emotions that are deeply rooted to the foundation of their relationship with God. A Christian martial artist has self-control, perseverance, focus and patience because the Holy Spirit has provided these as gifts. A Christian martial artist perseveres because he or she realizes God gives them the strength to endure. They are not random.

If we yield ourselves to God's will, and willingly conform to His purpose, He will empower us to overcome any obstacle. The Spirit wills the FOTS when we are prepared and ready to use them to help others. Galatians 5:16-18 says, "I say then: Walk in the Spirit, and you shall not fulfill the lust of the flesh. For the flesh lusts against the Spirit, and the Spirit against the flesh; and these are contrary to one another, so that you do not do the things that you wish. But if you are led by the Spirit, you are not under the law." We can see that a Spirit filled Christian martial artist does what is right not because of training hall etiquette, or from memorizing various martial arts creeds or tenants. A Christian martial artist does what is right because he or she has accepted the Holy Spirit into their lives and has been enriched and blessed by the FOTS.

In secular martial arts, the practitioner believes he or she has the fortitude to overcome obstacles internally. Therefore, they may not seek out God. The Christian martial artist realizes they are empowered by the Holy Spirit, and wisely given gifts which enrich our lives as we seek out God. It's a wonderful revelation to see students understand how intricately woven God can become in their training.

---

Now let's review scripture lessons that help define the Fruit of the Spirit, and how it pertains to a Christian martial artist:

**Love** – 'Even as the Father has loved me, so have I loved you: continue in my love. If you keep my commandments, and abide in his love; even as I have kept my Father's commandments, and abide in his love. These things I have spoken unto you, that my joy might remain in you, and that your joy might be full. This is my commandment: That you love one another as I have loved you." 1 John 4:16 says, "And so we know and rely on the love God has for us. God is love. Whoever lives in love lives in God, and God in him. Through Christ, our greatest goal is to do all things in love.

Love is defined by 1 Corinthians 13:4-8 above, which again also emphasizes attributes of a martial artist. ...Love is **patient,** love is **kind** *(courteous).* It does not envy, it does not boast, it is not **proud** *(humble).* It is not **rude**, it is not **self-seeking** *(humble),* it is not easily **angered** *(self-control),* it keeps no record of wrongs. Love does not delight in evil but rejoices with the truth. It always **protects**, always **trusts** *(integrity),* always hopes, always **perseveres** *(indomitable spirit).* LOVE NEVER FAILS...

**Joy** – "The joy of the Lord is your strength" (Nehemiah 8:10). "Let us fix our eyes on Jesus, the author and perfector of our faith, who for the joy set before him endured the cross, scorning its shame, and sat down at the right hand of the throne of God" (Hebrews 12:2). "Be joyful always; pray continually; *give thanks in all circumstances,* for this is God's will for you in Christ Jesus," 1Thessalonians 5:16-18.

### *Joy is Love's Strength*

**Peace** - "May the God of hope fill you with all joy and peace as you trust in him, so that you may overflow with hope by the power of the Holy Spirit" **(Romans 15:13)**

"Peace I leave with you, my peace I give unto you: Not as the world giveth, give I unto you. Let not your heart be troubled, neither let it be afraid" **(John. 14: 27).**

### *Peace is Love's Security*

**Patience** – "God will bring us back in countless ways to the same point over and over again. And He never tires of bringing us back to that one point until we learn the lesson, because His purpose is to produce the finished product. It may be a problem arising from our impulsive nature, but again and again, with the most persistent patience, God has brought us back to that one particular point." Oswald Chambers, "Becoming Entirely His (July 31),"

### *Patience is Love's Longevity*

**Faithfulness/ Self Control** - "But also for this very reason, giving all diligence, add to your faith virtue, to virtue knowledge, to knowledge self-control, to self-control perseverance, to perseverance godliness, to godliness brotherly kindness, and to brotherly kindness love"
(2 Peter 1:5-7).

The gift of faithfulness and self control is about enduring and about understanding God's unending love for us. It is often thought that we seek out God. In reality, it is God who waits patiently for us. We must commit to being faithful to him and controlling our own wants and desires to fully appreciate self control.

***Faithfulness is Love's Wisdom***

**Kindness/Goodness** - "We should live in purity, understanding, patience and kindness; in the Holy Spirit and in sincere love; in truthful speech and in the power of God; with weapons of righteousness in the right hand and in the left," (1 Thessalonians 1:11).

The gift of gentleness isn't about being unassertive, or indecisive. It is connected instead to a refusal to use power over anyone, unwillingness toward vengeance, spite or control. It is about building up instead of harming. There are gentle ways to be bold, non-violent ways to stand up for what is right, and martial arts can be the conduit for nurturing this gift.

***Goodness is Love's Character***

# ~ **Chapter 2** ~
# **Attributes of Christian Character**

The remaining chapters of the book are dedicated to lessons which can be used in the training hall. Chapter two focuses on the character attributes of a Christian. We must not only understand these character attributes, but we must put them to practice every day. If you don't practice martial arts on a daily basis, your technique will become less effective. Similarly, you must practice and hone your character every day. Make it razor sharp! How do you do this? First, start by making a plan of action. Decide each day that you will be an example to others by exemplifying the FOTS. Secondly, remember that you can't control other people, only your actions and words. The mark of a good person starts with realizing you can't control situations; you can only control the way you react to the experiences in your life.

## *Lesson 1 – Love Is Patient*

### I Corinthians 13: 4-8

"Love is patient, love is kind.  It does not envy, it does not boast, it is not proud.  It is not rude, it is not self-seeking, it is not easily angered, it keeps no record of wrongs.  Love does not delight in evil but rejoices with the truth.  It always protects, always trusts, always hopes, always perseveres.  Love never fails"

### Galatians 5:22-25

"But the fruit of the Spirit is love, joy, peace, patience, kindness, goodness, faithfulness, gentleness, and self-control. Against such things there is no law....If we live in the Spirit, let us also walk in the Spirit.  Let us not become conceited, provoking one another, or envying one another."

### Symbol

The symbol/image on the cover emphasizes the Fruit of the Spirit, which are the character attributes one should strive for as a Christian martial artist.  Specifically, the image is the Bible with two vines surrounding the cross of Jesus.  The vines are signified as Christ, "I am the vine, you are the branches," symbolizing our growth from biblical principles. Without the vine, we will wither and die.

## What does this mean to me?

No matter where we are in life – going to school, studying for a test, finding our first job, or getting ready for summer vacation, the Bible teaches us that we should "walk in the Spirit."

If someone wrongs you at school, forgive them. If someone needs help, go the extra mile to lend the person a helping hand. Remember the golden rule, "Do unto others as you would have them do unto you."

While learning martial arts techniques, often times it's easy to become overwhelmed and simply think you can't do something. It's the perseverance you attain that allows you to overcome these obstacles.

**After all, a black belt is a white belt who never gives up.**

## *Lesson 1 Review and Questions*

Why is it important for a Christian martial artist to remember and also practice the teachings in Galatians 5:22?

How can you show _____ toward your fellow martial artists, friends, family, etc?  (Inputs can be love, joy, peace, patience, kindness, goodness, faithfulness, self-control).

What does the symbol/cover image represent?

Name one of the tenants of martial arts teaching.
(Answer includes the Fruit of the Spirit, courtesy, integrity, perseverance, indomitable spirit).

According to I Corinthians 13: 4-8, "love never fails."  Please explain what this means to you.

Why is the "golden rule" so important for us to remember?

What is the significance of the words, "against such things there is no law?"

Prayer used after discussion:

Dear heavenly Father, I/we humbly come before you as your child/children, and ask that you help us be servant leaders to those around us.  Let us walk with peaceful hearts, loving others as you first loved us.  Remove that which holds us back from fully knowing you, so that we may do your work, exemplify the Fruit of the Spirit and become all you would have us be. Amen.

## *Lesson 2 – The Rock*

## Matthew 7: 24-27

"Therefore whoever hears these sayings of mine, and does them, I will liken him to a wise man who built his house on the rock: and the rain descended, the floods came, and the winds blew and beat on that house; and it did not fall, for it was founded on the rock.

But everyone who hears these saying of mine, and does not do them, will be like a foolish man who built his house on the sand: and the rain descended, the floods came, and the winds blew and beat on that house; and it fell. And great was its fall."

## What does this mean to me?

Ever wonder what it would be like to have all the knowledge and wisdom possible? To know your decisions were always correct and never questioned by others?

In school, everyone questions the repetitive actions of algebra class. In martial arts training, student's often get bored practicing form and proper stances.. A good foundation is important in every aspect of life. If you have a strong foundation, you can build upon it and know you are solid. In martial arts, a solid foundation allows a student to progress and master techniques more quickly.

Think about an athlete you look up to – a basketball star, Olympic athlete, etc., – they are looked up to by people because they have attained a level of excellence within their field. What most people don't realize is the determination and consistent building upon their foundational skills that has led them to be such a terrific athlete. Whether it's dribbling, shooting, sprinting, etc., they are relentless in their pursuit of perfection.

In everything you do, build a solid foundation!

School is often considered monotonous. At the time, doing math over and over again appears fruitless, but it truly helps you analyze situations in the real world! Practicing your stances and basic kicks allow you to master the flying kicks students want to learn – it all comes in time through building a solid foundation!

In the verse above, Christ is telling us to build our foundation upon Him. Trust and rely on Him, and your foundation will grow strong.

**Build your foundation for life on Christ!**

## *Lesson 2 Review and Questions*

What does Matthew 7: 24-27 mean to you?

What could the "rain, floods, and wind" represent in your own life?

How do you, in your life, insure a solid foundation?

Why is it important to build a solid foundation in martial arts?

Why is it important to listen and act upon what Christ's word tells us?

Why isn't it possible to master advanced martial arts techniques if a student hasn't learned basic skills?

How do you build a solid foundation with your friends, family, colleagues, etc?

Name an experience in your life where you didn't have a solid foundation. What would have happened if you had built your foundation strong?

Prayer used after discussion:

Dear heavenly Father, I/we come before you and ask for your wisdom. Allow us the wisdom and discernment to build a solid foundation for every part of our lives. Help us to rely upon you to weather the storms that may come, and be solid in our knowledge that only you can perfect us and our way. Thank you for first loving us. Amen

*Lesson 3 – Add to Your Faith*

**II Peter 1: 5-9**

"But also for this very reason, giving all diligence, add to your faith virtue, to virtue knowledge, to knowledge self-control, to self-control perseverance, to perseverance godliness, to godliness brotherly kindness, and to brotherly kindness love. For if these things are yours and abound, you will be neither barren nor unfruitful in the knowledge of our Lord Jesus Christ....for he who lacks these things is shortsighted, and has forgotten that he was cleansed from his old self."

Here are some great quotes about building your character:
"A spiritual life without discipline is impossible. Tighten your belt and go for it." "A man's quality of life is in direct relation to his commitment to excellence." "To get there, to win – your life needs discipline, order and arrangement."

**What does this mean to me?**

This verse of the Bible is talking about the persecution believers weathered for many years. Peter is talking about building one's internal character. To become all we can be, regardless of what we do in life – doctor, lawyer, fire man, clerk, martial arts instructor, we will only become all we can through Christ's help. He gives us the fuel to continue, to seek, to strive, to find, and not to yield!

Martial arts are well-known for its character building attributes. The amount of time alone to obtain black belt, let alone master instructor, takes decades of concentration, and focus on one's goal. One's character is challenged, and subsequently grows, when new challenges are overcome and confidence is built. I remember breaking my first brick. What a hurdle it was for me! Now, breaking bricks is no big deal, but the confidence it gave me realized I could push myself to new heights!

**I Peter 4:11b**

"Do things with the ability God supplies, that in all things God may be glorified through Jesus Christ."

**Rely upon Christ to build your character in order to become all you can be!**

## *Lesson 3 Review and Questions*

Why is it important we constantly build our character as Christ describes in the verses above?

What does (_____) mean to you? (inputs include faith, virtue, knowledge, self-control, perseverance, godliness, brotherly kindness, love).

What obstacles in your life have you overcome?  How did it build your character?

Why does the verse say, "He who has forgotten these things is shortsighted, and has forgotten that he was cleansed from his old self." What does this mean to you?

What does a strong character mean to you?

How do you continue to strengthen your character?

Is it possible to become all you can be if you don't focus on Christ?  Why or why not?

How can Christianity help strengthen your character as a martial artist?

Why is discipline so important in building your character?

Prayer used after discussion:

Dear heavenly Father, I/we come before you and thank you for the struggles presented to us. That we may grow closer to you through these experiences by understanding they grow our character. May you strengthen our minds, and our hearts, and allow us to be a light unto this world. May our actions toward others show love, godliness, self-control and thoughtfulness. Amen.

## *Lesson 4 Then Jesus Said to Them*

## Luke 22: 36

"Then Jesus said to them, 'But now, he who has a money bag, let him take it, and likewise a knapsack; and he who has no sword, let him sell his garment and buy one. For I say to you that this which is written must still be accomplished in Me...'"

## Context

This verse is describing Jesus' conversation with the disciples prior to being arrested by Judas and the guards. Jesus is preparing the disciples, telling them what is needed for the road ahead since he will shortly be arrested, judged, and crucified.

## What does this mean to me?

Christ told the disciples to purchase protection, a sword in this case, for the things to come. The sword is similar to your training in the martial arts. It is for defense only! The sword was used inappropriately by Peter, the disciple who cut the ear off an arresting guard.

Similarly, martial arts should never be used for offensive purposes. Use it to build your character, as a method to protect yourself and as a stepping stone to become closer to Christ. Practice martial arts with humility, self-control, kindness to your partner(s), gentleness, and patience as the Bible describes the Fruit of the Spirit. Allow martial arts to help foster a closer relationship to God, by studying the Bible and applying it to your life. Practice martial arts with diligence, perseverance, and self-control; giving honor and glory to God for the opportunity to learn something new, and develop new skills.

There is a famous quote which states, "Preach the gospel at all times, and if needed, use words." Allow your actions in and outside of the martial arts studio to build up others, Let others see you as an example of the Holy Spirit living within you.

**Focus your concentration on the goals He has set before you.**

## *Lesson 4 Review and Questions*

How is self-preservation and self-defense related to this verse?

Why are martial arts only used for defensive purposes?

Why did Christ tell the disciples to take their knapsack and purchase a sword?

Name one characteristic of Christian martial arts teachings. How does it differ from martial arts which focus on eastern religion?

How can you be an example outside of the martial arts studio to other people?

How do you describe the difference between Christian martial arts and other forms of self defense?

How can martial arts be used to build _____? (Inputs include character, self-control, perseverance, patience, godliness, humbleness)

Prayer used after discussion:

Dear heavenly Father, I/we thank you for the blessing of this class. We pray you will this class to bring us closer to you, and allow us to be more Christ-like in our actions toward others. Let your meekness, your kindness and gentleness live within us so we can be a light unto this world. Amen.

## *Lesson 5 - The Definition of Wisdom*

**How Do You Define Wisdom?** Is it your ability to apply knowledge (what you know)? Is it remembering experiences from the past to apply to current situations?

Regardless of how you define wisdom, true wisdom starts by living in God's will for your life.

**Why?** We are never complete unless God lives in us. It is utterly impossible for us to foresee everything, know all things, and be all things. Our omniscient Father steers us, and provides opportunities for us. Wouldn't it be better to live in God's will, and seek His understanding rather than rely upon ourselves? By focusing on God and seeking His will, we can find wisdom in the simple and redundant things in life.

**Proverbs 2: 6**
"For the Lord gives wisdom; from His mouth come knowledge and understanding."

**Proverbs 1:2-5**
"To know wisdom and instruction, to perceive the words of understanding, to receive the instruction of wisdom, justice, judgment, and equity; to give prudence to the simple, to the

young person knowledge and discretion – A wise man will hear and increase learning, and a man of understanding will attain wise counsel..."

## Context

How do you receive direction or instruction from others? In this class, the instructors are here to pass along their knowledge (understanding of skill and technique) and wisdom (ability to apply, or not apply, a certain technique in a specific situation).

In martial arts, as in life, wisdom does not equate to understanding instruction. It is what we do with the instruction that allows wisdom to flourish. The first step is to receive instruction to become wiser. The "equity" or attributes of wisdom include; good judgment, strong moral character, objectivity, and stability in our lives. Wisdom is truth and knowledge applied, not just knowing facts or information.

Whether in this class, at school, or on the job, it is important to receive instruction in the same manner. It allows you to grow, flourish and gain wisdom.

"Wisdom is the God-given ability to see life with rare objectivity and to handle life with rare stability." (*From Living on the Ragged Edge* by Charles Swindoll).

**Look to God for wisdom. Gaining wisdom is an adventure where God provides clarity, peace, and restfulness.**

## *Lesson 5 Review and Questions*

What is your definition of wisdom?

How is God's wisdom different than our own?

What is the difference between knowledge and discernment?

Why does God call us to rely upon Him rather than our own understanding?

Do you receive instruction with appreciation or frown upon it?

Why is it difficult to receive instruction from some people but not others?

How can you apply the following - a wise man speaks little and listens much, whereas a foolish man speaks much and listens little?

Prayer used after discussion:
Dear heavenly Father, I/we thank you for your guidance, your wisdom, and your caring. May we see things through your discretion and your wisdom. May we look to you, rather than ourselves, for understanding truth and wisdom. Amen.

## *Lesson 6 – The 5<sup>th</sup> Commandment*

### Exodus 20: 2 –

"Honor thy father and mother."

### Context

This is the 5<sup>th</sup> Commandment given by God to Moses in the Old Testament. Moses was to deliver the 10 commandments to His people so they would understand the laws set forth by God.

### What is the importance of this verse?

Throughout our lives, we are asked to respect authority, respect your elders, respect others privacy, etc. Respect is critical for a society to flourish. It is also critical to the success of a martial arts class. Without respect in the classroom, no one would learn – there would be disarray and no structure. Respect is something that is earned. It is difficult to truly respect someone simply because they say they deserve your respect!

There are varying types of respect:

**We ask you to respect each other** – focus on your technique rather than distracting the class.

**We ask you to respect yourselves** – Having a clean uniform and presenting yourself correctly shows you have respect for yourself.

**The instructors respect each other** – for the accomplishments, goals, and help they provide to each other and students.

**Respect in this class starts with the instructors**. When you see us working together, you see us respect each other by bowing to one another, to you, or by remaining silent while another instructor speaks.

**We ask you to respect the instructors** – Your instructor(s) have many years of martial arts instruction.. Respecting each instructor for their knowledge, willingness to help, and previous accomplishments, allows everyone to be on the same "playing field" – we all respect each other.

**Where does this lead us?**
Respect for others must first start by respecting ourselves. Knowing your limitations and what's right and wrong. Coincidently, respecting your father and mother brings you respect from them.

Respecting your father and mother allows you to learn to respect yourself and other people. Ask God to plant a seed of respect in your heart for those around you – it may change the way you view other people!

## *Lesson 6 Review and Questions*

Why is it important to understand each of the commandments?

The wording used in many of the commandments appears outdated. How are the commandments still relevant in today's society?

Describe your life without respect for others and from other people!

Why do people argue about having the Ten Commandments publicly displayed?

How can you show respect for your parents, colleagues, fellow martial artists?

How does respecting your parents and peers help you?

How do you show respect for yourself?

Prayer used after discussion:
Dear heavenly Father, I/we thank you for the structure and order you bring to our lives. We pray you would plant a new seed of respect in our hearts. Allow us to respect those around

us, and find a new level of understanding for our family and friends. Thank you for being our example, and for loving us. Amen.

## *Lesson 7 – Defining Success*

### How do you define success?

Is it winning every contest or activity? Is it having the best car, most money, or most possessions? Or, perhaps, is your definition of success your ability to "never fail?"

### Why?

Defining success must start with accepting the possibility of failure. If you want to succeed, you must be willing to fail. Success must also be defined from within, not by outward possessions or things you acquire. There will always be someone with more money, a nicer car, or a larger house. Striving for possessions will always leave you wanting more. It will be a fruitless attempt at finding a pseudo-success or happiness that does not exist.

In 1927 Babe Ruth hit 60 home runs, which was more than anyone in the history of baseball. He also set another record that year: He struck out more than anyone in the history of baseball! The truth is, if you want to hit home runs, you have to be willing to strike out too!

## Context

In martial arts, a person must be willing to accept change. Furthermore, a person must be willing to fail a few times in order to succeed. There are times in everyone's training where a person will not succeed. We learn and become better through our failures! We remain complacent through our successes. In this class, you must do everything with the utmost effort, knowing through any failure you will find success!

Thomas Edison, who is well known for his many inventions, once said, "Show me a thoroughly satisfied person and I will show you a failure!" Don't forget, this comes from a man who persevered through 2500 attempts at making a light bulb work correctly! He was quoted as saying, "I don't see my attempts as failure! Inventing the light bulb provided me 2500 ways to perfect my invention!"

Goethe, a great thinker and philosopher once said, "Treat people as they are, and they will remain the same. Treat them as though they were what they can be, and we help them become what they are capable of becoming." In this class, the instructors don't see you as white belts, yellow belts, or brown belts. We see each student's training as a progression of successes and failures which eventually lead to obtaining a black belt.  Don't be afraid to fail, it's the only way to gain true success.

**Understand that successes and failures will pass in time.  Learning from our experiences, and not being afraid to fail, allows us to succeed!**

## *Lesson 7 Review and Questions*

How do you define success?

Why are people afraid to fail?

What can we do to overcome the fear of failure?

Why can't a person find true happiness or success through possessions?

Why must you be willing to fail in order to find true success?

Name something you initially failed at, only to succeed upon consistent effort and focus?

Prayer used after discussion:

Dear heavenly Father, I/we thank you for the challenges and struggles in our lives. Allow us to understand that during difficult times in our lives, You are there with us, guiding us to succeed. Father, we ask you to help us overcome our fear of failure, and build in us a heart of confidence that we can succeed at anything with your help. Amen.

# ~ **Chapter 3** ~

# **Disciplining Your Mind & Body**

Throughout this chapter, the lessons will focus on scripture versus that help discipline your mind and body. In martial arts, training the mind is just as important as training the body. You may be physically capable of breaking a stack of bricks, but if your mind isn't fit for the task, you will not be able to accomplish it. It is the same with our Christianity. Whether its understanding where balance begins, using the triple filter test, doing things deliberately, or being fit to bear fruit for God's kingdom, we must strive to train ourselves to be physically and mentally fit for the challenges this world provides. Rejoice when you are challenged, for it is an opportunity to learn and excel!

## Lesson 8 – Whatever You Do, Do Well

### Ecclesiastes 9:10

"Whatever you do, do well. For when you go to the grave, there will be no work or planning or knowledge or wisdom."

### 1 Corinthians 9:24-27

"Remember that in a race everyone runs, but only one person gets the prize. You also must run in such a way that you will win. All athletes practice strict self control. They do it to win a prize that will fade away, but we do it for an eternal prize. So I run straight to the goal with purpose in every step. I am not like a boxer who misses his punches. I discipline my body like an athlete, training it to do what it should. Otherwise, I fear that after preaching to others I myself might be disqualified."

### Context

Our study of the martial arts is similar. We need to discipline our bodies and minds. If we could test without meeting certain qualifications, or pass every test without difficulty, what would we be learning? After a few years of testing, we would have a piece of paper indicating a belt rank. We would not have the skill nor the understanding of martial arts technique and philosophy to have truly attained black belt. However, if, after many years of pushing ourselves to be better, striving for relentless perfection of technique, we would have a black belt with all the knowledge and skill such a rank entails.

## What does this mean to me in this class?

Discipline your body to quickly and instinctively do the things you have taught it. Discipline the mind in like fashion. A well-disciplined martial artist (AND CHRISTIAN) has instincts of doing right because of prior determination, perseverance, and practice.

These versus remind me of an experience I had in my previous training hall. There was a beginning student who apparently had been shown a variety of technique – from a 360 degree spin kick, to a running / jump side kick. His enthusiasm was terrific, his excitement about martial arts was without question. But the discipline in his technique was no where to be found. Spinning, spinning and spinning he went, around the training hall floor from side to side doing jump side kicks to impress whoever was in the training hall. He literally looked more like a person at a "grunge" concert throwing himself all over the place.

If you don't discipline your mind and body to develop your techniques, you'll be like this student who had skill beyond his belt rank, but had no understanding of what he was doing, when to do it, or how to ask for help.

**Don't ever give up on your goal. Allow God to guide you to His purpose and calling for your life, and you will find fulfillment and peace.**

## *Lesson 8 Review and Questions*

What does the verse above say about work, planning, knowledge and wisdom?

Why is it important to "do well in whatever you do?"

What is the eternal prize we strive to obtain as Christian martial artists?

How can you obtain this eternal prize in every class?

Why is it important to discipline your body and mind each day?

What can we learn from the student in the story above, who was shown advanced techniques but had not acquired the skill to adequately demonstrate them?

How is our relationship with Christ sometimes like the story above?

Prayer used after discussion:

Dear heavenly Father, I/we thank you for bringing purpose into our lives. We ask that you help us to find your purpose in every walk of our life, and that you would guide our decisions based on your wisdom and understanding, and not our own. Use our training to make our focus and concentration razor sharp, that we may live according to your word. Amen.

## *Lesson 9 – Where is the Balance?*

In today's fast-paced society, we often feel overwhelmed. "Information overload" is a common term used; there is too much to process, too much to remember, too much to do and too many responsibilities placed on us. Balance in all aspects of our lives is a key to living a full, healthy life.

Having good balance for martial arts techniques is simple to understand. If you have it, you're able to execute a technique with power, stability, and proper focus and control. Balance in martial arts, as in life, goes beyond honing skills and setting appropriate boundaries. Balance is not an arrival point, it is today's decision.

Balance is the sum of all the Fruit of the Spirit. You cannot show love, joy, peace, patience, kindness, goodness, faithfulness, gentleness, and self-control, unless you have balance in your life. The Fruit of the Spirit, like balance, are seeds that are planted early on in our "development." Under proper care and nurturing, balance becomes part of our everyday life. Our training in martial arts begins and ends with balance. Why should it be any different in our daily life?

Balance can begin with remembering God's commandments! God's fourth commandment is to remember the Sabbath. It is also a principle we ought to live by; to remove one-self from being too busy. This principle reminds us to focus on the important things in life, rather than becoming restless inside and stressed.

In martial arts, balance is a skill you acquire. Advanced techniques challenge your "state of balance," and allow you to hone your skill as you overcome "balance obstacles." In life, you must decide a head of time on the basics to creating balance. It is deciding what is important rather than urgent. This decision will allow you peace, and provide an anchor to flourish the Fruit of the Spirit.

Finding balance in life starts with studying the Word. Balance is understanding what God is doing right now to show you peace.

**Balance begins with a yearning for God to anchor your life and all your decisions.**

## *Lesson 9 Review and Questions*

What does good balance do for a Christian? A martial artist?

How are the two above similar? How do they differ?

Why should we remember the Sabbath?

What brings your life into balance?

What gives you peace?

What are the balance obstacles you must overcome in life? In your martial arts training?

Prayer used after discussion:
Dear heavenly Father, I/we thank you for the balance you bring to our lives. Thank you for the example you set before us, by remembering your commandments and reminding us balance is a daily decision to do what is right. Father, we ask you to increase our capacity for balance, that we may overcome more through the understanding of your word and help others as they find balance in their lives. Amen.

## *Lesson 10 – Your Body is a Temple*

### I Corinthians 6: 19-20

"You surely know that your body is a temple where the Holy Spirit lives. The Spirit is in you and is a gift from God."

### Romans 6:13

"Give yourselves to God, as people who have been raised from death to life. Make every part of your body a slave that pleases God."

### Context

We should take care of ourselves, not only for our own physical well-being, but because we are temples of God. If we are not "fit" physically or mentally, we are incapable of becoming all we can be. In this class, we spend our time and energy physically training for spiritual fitness. We wear our uniform of purity and belt of truth as the Bible says (armor of God).

What we do with our bodies is what we do with our souls. What we think about reflects who we are. Because of this, we must discipline and protect our minds.

**Martial Arts**

The outward, physical attributes of what we learn are often easier to see than how we are growing mentally. By now you are probably aware of the increase in flexibility, increased aerobic capacity, or loss of weight or gain of muscle. What's less noticeable is your circulation has improved, improved muscular coordination, reflex action, and awareness.

Something I enjoy watching is the transformation that takes place when a new student puts on his or her training uniform, and begins learning techniques. People find new confidence, the shyness and timid-ness tend to disappear. The students take a role of responsibility and authority for learning techniques, and mastering movements.

Our hope as instructors is you never lose sight of the reason why we are all here – to "bear fruit" or share God's word. It starts by being physically and mentally fit – guarding our minds, and increasing our abilities both physically and spiritually.

**May God guide and bless you as you increase your physical ability, and may He bless you richly through the understanding of His word**.

## *Lesson 10 Review and Questions*

Why is it important to stay fit physically and mentally?

What benefits have you seen by staying fit through your training?

What benefits have you noticed by reading your Bible daily?

How are the physical attributes of martial arts training similar to the internal development of our mental and spiritual growth through our understanding of Christ?

Being mentally fit means being able to defend our minds against evil and wrong doing. How do you protect against this in your life?

How is "bearing fruit" for Christ similar to increased circulation, muscle growth, and flexibility?

Prayer used after discussion:
Dear heavenly Father, I/we thank you for the opportunity to glorify you in this class. Help us to discipline our minds and bodies to be soldiers for Christ. We pray you would strengthen

us as the Spirit lives within us, molding us into the person Christ desires. Amen.

## *Lesson 11 – Who Created Evil?*

The university professor challenged his students with this question.

"Did God create everything that exists?" A student bravely replied, "Yes, he did!" "God created everything?" The professor asked. "Yes sir", the student replied.

The professor answered, "If God created everything, then God created evil, since evil exists, and according to the principle that our works define who we are, then God is evil".

The student became quiet before such an answer. The professor, quite pleased with himself, boasted to the students that he had proven once more that the Christian faith was a myth.

Another student raised his hand and said, "Can I ask you a question, professor?" "Of course", replied the professor. The student stood up and asked, "Professor, does cold exist?" "What kind of question is this? Of course it exists. Have you never been cold?" The students snickered at the young man's question.

The young man replied, "In fact sir, cold does not exist. According to the laws of physics, what we consider cold is in reality the absence of heat. Every body or object is susceptible to study when it has or transmits energy, and heat is what makes a body or matter have or transmit energy. Absolute zero (-460° F) is the total absence of heat; all matter becomes inert and incapable of reaction at that temperature. Cold does not exist. We have created this word to describe how we feel if we have no heat."

The student continued, "Professor, does darkness exist?" The professor responded, "Of course it does."

The student replied, "Once again you are wrong sir, darkness does not exist either. Darkness is in reality the absence of light. Light we can study, but not darkness. In fact we can use Newton's prism to break white light into many colors and study the various wavelengths of each color. You cannot measure darkness. A simple ray of light can break into a world of darkness and illuminate it. How can you know how dark a certain space is? You measure the amount of light present. Isn't this correct? Darkness is a term used by man to describe what happens when there is no light present."

Finally the young man asked the professor, "Sir, does evil exist?"

Now uncertain, the professor responded, "Of course as I have already said. We see it every day. It is in the daily example of man's inhumanity to man. It is in the multitude of crime and violence everywhere in the world. These manifestations are nothing else but evil."

To this the student replied, "Evil does not exist sir, or at least it does not exist unto itself. Evil is simply the absence of God. It is just like darkness and cold, a word that man has created to describe the absence of God. God did not create evil. Evil is not like faith, or love that exist just as does light and heat. Evil is the result of what happens when man does not have God's love present in his heart. It's like the cold that comes when there is no heat or the darkness that comes when there is no light."

The professor sat down.

The young man's name --- Albert Einstein

## Lesson 11 Review and Questions

What is evil?

Did God create evil?

How is evil similar to cold and darkness?

How are faith and love similar to light and heat?

Why is it important to have God's love present in our hearts?

In martial arts training, how do you nurture faith, love, patience and self-control?

Prayer used after discussion:
Dear heavenly Father, I/we thank you for being the light to our lives. We thank you for giving us the choice of living in your will and freely giving your Holy Spirit to live within us. May we see this world through your kindness and mercy. Help us to show others the faith and love you first showed us. Amen.

## *Lesson 12 – Do Not Despise One of These*

### Matthew 18: 10 – 14

"Take heed that you do not despise one of these little ones...For the Son of Man has come to save that which was lost. What do you think? If a man has a hundred sheep, and one of them goes astray, does he not leave the ninety-nine and go to the mountains to seek the one that is straying? And if he should find it, assuredly, I say to you, he rejoices more over that sheep than over the others remaining. Even so it is not the will of your Father who is in heaven that one of these little ones should perish."

### Context

Jesus is talking about His people. Jesus is stating every sheep, or person, is important. Interestingly, Christ story resembles our relationship with Him. We often consider ourselves the one to eventually seek God out, but in reality it is Christ who is there with open arms waiting for us.

### What does this mean?

We are all equally valuable to God. No one is useless to Him. Not a child, not the unattractive, not the clumsy, not the tired, not the discouraged. God uses His children.

Our value isn't based on the amount of money we have, the number of friends we have, the car we drive, whether we start on the team at school, what martial arts belt we wear, or whether we're a director, VP, or a CEO of a company.

Similarly, in martial arts – you'll probably get "lost" a few times. You won't understand the technique, if there's a chamber position, or where your balance is supposed to be when applying a technique. Like Christ, the instructors are here to help you "get back on track" and feel re-assured that you're on the right path.

We all belong to God's eternal plan. There is an eternal purpose. You may not know it now, but God is always there for you, regardless of whether you go astray or not. Be confident in knowing God never turns His back on you.

**God's future plans are brought out by the present vision of His people.**

## *Lesson 12 Review and Questions*

What are the similarities between our relationship with God and a sheep becoming lost?

What is significant about the words above, "Take heed that you do not despise one of these little ones?"

Why is it important to know that it is God who seeks us out similar to the shepherd in the story above?

Why do people often associate their status with the things acquired rather than on the relationships a person has developed?

Think of an experience in your martial arts training where you felt lost. What did the instructor or fellow students do to help you get back on track?

How can you help others who feel lost get back on track?

Prayer used after discussion:
Dear heavenly Father, I/we thank you for the gift of your son who came to this world so we could spend eternity with you. Thank you for always having open arms, for caring enough

about each of us individually that you would seek us out. Dear Lord, we ask that you would allow us to understand your sense of kindness and gentleness, that we may be an example to others. Amen.

## *Lesson 13 – Ask God to Bless Everyone*

## Romans 12:14-18 (Contemporary Christian Version – CEV)

"Ask God to bless everyone who mistreats you. Ask him to bless them and not to curse them. When others are happy, be happy with them, and when they are sad, be sad. Be friendly with everyone. Don't be proud and feel that you are smarter than others. Make friends with ordinary people. Don't mistreat someone who has mistreated you. But try to earn the respect of others, AND DO YOUR BEST TO LIVE AT PEACE WITH EVERYONE."

## Context

Note the scripture above says "do your best." Another translation says, "If it be possible, as much as lieth in you, live peaceably with all men (KJV). As we all know, it may not always be possible to live at peace with all men. Look at today's world – there are groups around the world that don't like you and me, not because of anything we've done, but simply because of who we are or our beliefs. Although others may not like us for one reason or another, that is not an excuse for us to give up hope, or stop loving them. There is a saying, "hate the sin, love the sinner." As Christians, we must live by this creed.

**Martial Arts**

It may be hard to believe when first beginning this class, but the martial arts absolutely comprise love, among the other Fruit of the Spirit. The martial arts began thousands of years ago because people were not given the right to defend themselves or their belongings. Thus, people began using farm equipment as well as honing their own bodies in order to protect themselves.

By now you ought to know that victory is actually avoiding conflict, and finding peace with others rather than defeating them. In Luke 6:29, the Bible says, "If someone slaps you on the cheek, don't stop that person from slapping you on the other cheek. If someone wants to take your coat, don't try and keep back your shirt (CEV).

Luke 6:32 - "If you love only someone who loves you, will God praise you for that?" Luke 6:36 - "but love your enemies and be good to them."

What would this world be like if everyone who heard these words actually lived by them? Start first with yourself, by doing what is right. Do things deliberately, with meaning and taking action to do what you have been taught. Start tomorrow – at the very least do one thing for another person - maybe someone you don't agree with, or someone you don't understand, etc.

**Like people for their qualities, love them for the faults.**

## *Lesson 13 Review and Questions*

Why is it important to ask God to bless those that mistreat you?

How can contempt and mistrust ruin a relationship with others? With God?

Why are the words, "slap on the cheek" often misinterpreted as being docile or non-confrontational?

Why is it important not return insult for insult?

Is it true or false, that if you find yourself in a confrontation, you have already lost? What is the best way to avoid a verbal or physical confrontation?

Why is it sometimes impossible to live at peace with all people?

As a martial artist, why is it important to do things deliberately, always accompanying decisions with actions and finishing what you start?

Prayer used after discussion:

Dear heavenly Father, I/we thank you for your words of wisdom and guidance. Father, we ask you to help us live at peace with others, to love those that dislike us and be friendly with everyone. Father, in this world of hatred and disgust, may we be a light unto this world. Allow our faith, love, joy and kindness extend to others that they may see you within us. Amen.

## Lesson 14 – The Triple Filter Test

In ancient Greece (469 - 399 BC), Socrates was well known for his wisdom.

One day the great philosopher came upon an acquaintance who said excitedly, "Socrates, do you know what I just heard about one of your students?"

"Wait a moment," Socrates replied. "Before telling me anything I would like you to pass a little test. It's called the Triple Filter Test."

"Triple filter?"

"That's right," Socrates continued. "Before you talk to me about my student, it might be a good idea to take a moment and filter what you're going to say. The first filter is Truth. Have you made absolutely sure that what you are about to tell me is true?"

"No," the man said, "actually I just heard about it and ..."

"All right," said Socrates. "So you don't really know if it's true or not. Now let's try the second filter, the filter of Goodness. Is what you are about to tell me about my student something good?"

"Well, no, on the contrary..."

"So," Socrates continued, "you want to tell me something bad about him, but you're not certain it's true. You may still pass the test though, because there's one filter left: the filter of Usefulness. Is what you want to tell me about my student going to be useful to me?"

"No, I suppose it isn't really."

"Well," concluded Socrates, "if what you want to tell me is neither true nor good nor even useful, why tell it to me at all?"

## *Lesson 14 Review and Questions*

What is the triple filter test?

Why is it important to remember the triple filter test prior to saying something about another person?

What does the Bible say about our speech and our tongue?

What is significant about the "triple filter test" and gossiping with others?

In your martial arts training, how can you relate to the "true, good and useful" the lesson above discusses while practicing your technique?

How can you be an example to someone who may say something untrue, bad, or useless about another person?

As Christians, how does God call us to interact with others in our speech and actions?

Prayer used after discussion:
Dear heavenly Father, I/we thank you for the wisdom found in your word. Father, we ask that you guard our hearts, minds,

actions and words so they may only be true, good, and useful toward other people. Help us to understand our words have great impact on other people. May our words always uplift, always love, and always rejoice with others as found in I Corinthians 13. Amen

## *Lesson 15 – Is Pain My Punishment?*

Sometimes people question God – "Is pain my punishment?" You've heard the expression "The rain falls on the just and the unjust" – or better, the unjust and the unjust, for we are all sinners. All of us are or will be victims of pain – it's an unfortunate fact of our existence, regardless of how good or bad we are. Fortunately, there is one who knows, and understands that pain.

Years from now, we may realize that it was those struggles that taught us something we could not have otherwise learned...there was a purpose in our pain. Some things can be taught, others must be lived to be understood.

Consider the pain Christ endured while hear on earth...suffering and dying for us, on our behalf! Having kids of my own I often think of whether I could give my children away for a greater good – I know I'm human, because there's no way I would!

Think of the teen-age professional surfer who was attacked by a shark in 2004 and lost her arm. The entire time they were taking her out of the water, into the ambulance, and at the hospital – she was professing her faith. She took that painful situation and made it glorify God – in fact, shortly after recuperating in the hospital, she was on national television. Once again, she professed her faith and her love for Christ. She is a light unto this world!

From this example, we can see God's purpose is greater than our pain in any given situation. He has a greater purpose than a particular problem you may be dealing with. Always know God will bring you through tough times – for His purpose is greater than any dilemma we may face.

**Glorify God in all times and all places, knowing His purpose envelopes us all.**

## *Lesson 15 Review and Questions*

Is God the cause of our pain?

Why do so many people think God directly causes pain, or unhappiness, etc?

How can you give God glory and praise even in the most difficult of times?

Discuss a painful experience in your life that eventually led to something much more revealing (possibly part of God's plan for you or others).

How did God use the young, teenage surfer, who lost her arm, to bring hope and glory to the situation?

How can you be an example to others, or bring happiness through sorrow?

Prayer used after discussion:
Dear heavenly Father, I/we glorify you for the love and hope you bring us.  Father, we ask you to help us find peace, strength and encouragement in difficult times, that we may see your purpose rather than focus on our own difficulties.  May we

be a light unto this world by bringing glory and honor to you in all times and all places.  Amen.

## *Lesson 16 – Guard Your Minds*

### I Peter 1: 13, 15, 16

"Therefore guard your minds, and rest your hope fully upon the grace that is to be brought to you at the revelation of Jesus Christ; as obedient children, not conforming yourselves to the former lives; but be as He who called you is holy, you also be holy in all your conduct, because it is written, 'Be holy, for I am holy.'"

### I Thessalonians 5: 16 – 18

"Rejoice always, pray without ceasing, in everything give thanks; for this is the will of God in Christ Jesus for you. Test all things; hold fast what is good. Abstain from every form of evil."

### I Peter 4: 11b

"...that in all things God may be glorified through Jesus Christ, to whom belong the glory and honor forever and ever." Proverbs 18:21 says, "Approach everything with a positive attitude."

### Context

These versus are talking about finding JOY. While joy is normally associated with happiness, the type of joy described in the Bible is something more. Joy does not vanish when things take a turn for the worse; it endures, even during the worst of times. True joy does not come by circumstances; it comes from deep within. We are joyful because we recognize God has solutions to our problems.

**What does this mean to me?** In these verses, God is telling us that regardless of our circumstances, or how rough things are, we should give glory and honor to God and have joy. Joy and happiness through "happenings" do not sustain us. Sustained joy and happiness occur through knowing and living in God's will and having a personal relationship with Him.

Finding sustaining joy is often easier said than done. During difficult times in our lives it's human to feel overwhelmed, as if there's no way out, or the only way to get through a situation is doing something contrary to what we've been taught.

God calls us to reach out to Him during these times. Remember, Christ prayed to His Father just moments before the guards came and took Him away to be judged. He said, "Not my will, but thy will be done." Christ new His mission was to bring everlasting joy to His people.

**Consistent, unwavering and sustainable joy is only found when we seek God's will.**

## Lesson 16 Review and Questions

How can it be possible to give thanks in every situation, in particular when things aren't going well?

What does, "not conforming yourselves to your former lives" mean to you?

How can a positive attitude help you find joy?

What is the joy the verse above is talking about?

How is the joy Christ hopes for us different than how the world views joy?

How is your life, and the joy you have different now that Christ lives in you?

How have you been able to bring enduring joy to someone else? How did it affect the other person?

Prayer used after discussion:

Dear heavenly Father, I/we give you thanks and praise for giving us eternal life. Lord, we ask that you would bless us with consistent and unwavering joy that only comes through knowing your will for our lives,. Help us to find joy in every part of our lives and our daily routines, that we may see you in all things. Amen.

## *Lesson 17 – Put On the Breast Plate*

### I Thessalonians 5:8-10

"Put on the breastplate of faith and love, and as a helmet the hope of salvation. For God did not appoint us to wrath, but to obtain salvation through our Lord Jesus Christ, who died for us, that whether we wake or sleep, we should live together with Him."

### Ephesians 6: 13-18

"Therefore take up the whole armor of God, that you may be able to withstand in the evil day, and having done all, to stand. Stand therefore, having girded your waist with truth, having put on the breastplate of righteousness, and having worn your feet with the gospel of peace; above all, taking the shield of faith with which you will be able to quench all the fiery darts of evil. And take the helmet of salvation, and the sword of the Spirit, which is the word of God; praying always with all prayer in the Spirit." The armor of God gives Christians victory over sin and protection from the devil.

### Context

The Armor of God consists of six pieces of equipment. Much like martial arts techniques and training, these pieces of equipment must be used and put into practice regularly in order to be effective. During class shut down (for the holidays), I'm sure you find your technique isn't as razor sharp as during consistent practice. Just as you practice your martial art technique daily, you must also learn to wear God's armor each day. Times of trial will become more easily dealt with because you are consistently razor sharp, and prepared with God's protection.

**Belt of truth** - John 8:32, 14:6, Psalms 51:6 **Body Armor of righteousness** - Isaiah 59:17, Matthew 6:33, Proverbs 11:4, 12:28

**Shoes of peace** – Luke 1:79, Romans 8:6, 10:15, Isaiah 52:7, Colossians 3:15

**Shield of faith** – James 2:17, Hebrews 11:3, 2 Timothy 4:7, Galatians 3:26

**Helmet of salvation** – Psalms 27:1, 62:2 Romans 1:16

**Sword of the spirit** – Philippians 1:19, Hebrews 4:12, Romans 8:14

**What does this mean to me?**

Have you ever had a bad day at school or work? The morning just starts wrong and the whole day seems to get more difficult? This scripture helps us to understand that our lives won't always be simple, but God calls us to "wear the armor" to withstand those difficult times in our lives. Notice that every area of a person's body is armored!

When things are tough, or things just aren't going our way, look to Christ to comfort you. The armor described in these verses means to be ready for those bad days or tough times in our life and allow Christ to protect us by being righteous, truthful, peaceful, and faithful to Him in all we do and say!

**Next time you get ready for the day, consider "getting ready" by allowing Christ to strengthen you with His armor!**

## *Lesson 17 Review and Questions*

Why is it important to wear the armor of God?  How does it protect you during your day?

What significance does "faith, hope and love" have in this verse?

What could happen if you didn't prepare each day by wearing God's armor?

How can a martial arts uniform, sparring gear and the tenants of martial arts be likened to the armor of God?

What is the significance of wearing a white uniform in martial arts class?  How can it be considered similar to the holy armor of God?

Name an experience where you had to choose to do the right thing, and how doing so protected you from evil?

Prayer used after discussion:
Dear heavenly Father, I/we thank you for sending your son to bring us salvation.  We ask that you would help us to prepare

each day with righteousness, peace and the knowledge you are always there, protecting us and watching over us.  Amen.

## *Lesson 18 – Then David Said. . .*

### I Samuel 17: 45 - 47

"Then David said to the Philistine (Goliath), "You come to me with a sword, with a spear, and with a javelin. But I come to you in the name of the Lord of hosts, the God of the armies of Israel, whom you have defied. This day the Lord will deliver you into my hand...Then all this assembly shall know that the Lord does not save with sword and spear; for the battle is the Lord's, and He will give you into our hands..."

### Context

This verse is speaking of the shepherd boy, David, who met the huge Philistine giant, Goliath. Goliath was a nine foot tall warrior, who had been sent to destroy David and his army. David, armed with only a sling and 5 smooth stones, destroyed Goliath and his Philistine army.

### What does this mean?

There are certain things people know not to do...don't fight a lion with a toothpick, you don't stand in traffic and cross the street, and you don't send a boy to destroy a warrior! The King at the time was Saul, who was out of options, so he sent David to meet this warrior.

It is when we are out of options that we are most ready for God's surprises. God certainly made his point from the story above! The soldiers gasped, Goliath jeered, David whipped his stone.

Whenever you are confronted with a huge problem, or something in life that just seems too "Goliath" to contend with – lean on God, and allow him to surprise you!

Similarly, in martial arts, there will be times in the future where you'll need to perfect a technique, or participate in sparring with a larger opponent, or even compete at a tournament! Don't let the size of the challenge lead you astray – stand firm and know all things are possible with God.

**Rely upon God to conquer the "Goliath" in your life – persevere and allow him to surprise you!**

## *Lesson 18 Review and Questions*

Why do you think God chose David, a shepherd boy, to stand up and eventually defeat a massive warrior?

What is significant about David's smooth stones and sling versus Goliath's armor and spear?

Why was David so confident?  How did his confidence change the war against the Philistines?

What challenges in your life made you feel like "David vs. Goliath?"

When have you felt you were only armed with only a sling? What became of the situation?

Prayer used after discussion:

Dear heavenly Father, I/we are humbled by your miracles.  You sent David to defeat a war hero, and made David a hero unto your people.  Father, we pray you would bless us with the confidence and belief of David – that you will provide for your people and give them the skills to overcome the obstacles in their lives.  Amen.

## *Lesson 19 – When He Had Called the People*

### Mark 8: 34 – 37

"When He had called the people to Himself, with His disciples also, He said to them, 'Whoever desires to come after Me, let him deny himself, and take up his cross, and follow Me. For whoever desires to save his life will lose it, but whoever loses his life for My sake and the gospel's will save it. For what will it profit a man if he gains the whole world, and loses his own soul? Or what will a man give in exchange for his soul?'"

### Context

Jesus is talking to the people of Jerusalem before he is taken away to be crucified. He is telling us we will lose our lives if we try and save it. He wants us to focus on Him and do His will. "Take up his cross" means to deny ourselves of the concerns of this world and set our sites on Christ.

### What does this mean?

Jesus is telling us we need to live for Him. To be content with what He has given us, and not strive to grasp the world in our hands. In our lives we may have a lesser paying job than many, or we may have difficulty in school in comparison to our classmates. Jesus is calling us to "pick up our cross and follow

Him." He wants us to put our burdens on Him. Allow Him to carry us in difficult times.

Similarly, a black belt or any martial artist must give him/herself up to gain. You give up those things which hinder you from becoming your best. Part of the creed of martial arts is, "I pledge to develop myself in a positive manner, and avoid anything that would reduce my physical health or mental growth." You persevere through tough times, work extra hard on a kick or hand technique until you've finally mastered it. It's all part of the process. It's only at this point in martial arts that you have obtained patience, peace, joy, self-control, and perseverance.

A Christian must also give him / herself up to Christ to gain eternal life, and what God has in store for us as His children.

**Allow God to create a path in your life, and desire to do His will in every walk of life.**

## *Lesson 19 Review and Questions*

What is the great commission, and why are all of us commanded to take up our cross and follow Christ?

How can a person save his or her life by denying themselves of earthly treasures and the things of this world?

Why do you think so many people focus on earthly treasures and what can be acquired rather than on intrinsic qualities such as humbleness, generosity, patience, etc.?

Why does the world see contentment as a trap?

Why is it important to find contentment in our lives? How does this help us focus on Christ?

What must you give up as a martial artist, or more importantly, as a Christian, to become what God wants for you?

Prayer used after discussion:
Dear heavenly Father, I/we thank you for your undeserving love. We pray you would give us the courage to daily deny ourselves of worldly concerns, and to pick up our cross and follow you. We thank you for carrying our burdens, and ask

that you would give us the strength to cast our doubts and concerns upon you, rather than carry them on our shoulders. Amen.

# Chapter 4

# ~ Being a Person of Action ~

Throughout this chapter, you will find numerous examples of being a person of action. In martial arts, a tenant of teaching is, "always accompany decisions with actions, and always finish what you start." The following lessons focus on the multitude of spiritual gifts and their use to enrich people's lives, understanding the definition of meekness, and realizing God calls each of us to bring His word to the world. Being a Christian starts with knowing Christ and understanding He died for us. Now that He lives in us, God calls us to pick up our cross and follow Him. In other words, bring the good news to all people. May you find an example that fans your internal flame. An example that allows you to take action!

## Lesson 20 – I Have Glorified You

### John 17: 4b

"I have glorified You on the earth. I have finished the work which You have given Me to do...."

### Luke 22: 39 – 44

"Coming out, Jesus went to the Mount of Olives...and He knelt down and prayed, saying, 'Father, if it is Your will, take this cup away from Me; nevertheless not My will, but Yours, be done.' And being in agony, He prayed more earnestly.'"

### Context

These two verses are describing Jesus prayers to His Father in heaven. Christ new His mission on earth. At the Mount of Olives he left His disciples to pray that God's will be done, even though Jesus new it meant dying for all people so that eternity with Him would be possible.

### What Does This Mean?

Have you ever been asked to do something you didn't want to do? Or, have you ever been put in a position where you didn't think you could accomplish the task, or the goal?

Just imagine if Jesus hadn't completed His mission, or followed His Father's will!  It would mean all of us would not have a choice to be with Him forever!  But through His example, we can certainly accomplish anything set in front of us.

What is your mission?  To get an "A" in class, to be a testimony to others around you?  To act upon what God calls you to do in all areas of your life at home and at school or work?

Martial arts asks much of a person – your time, commitment, focus, among other things.   In return, it provides an opportunity for you to reach a goal – a black belt.  In similar fashion, pray each day that Christ will provide an outline for you in your life, and pray as Jesus did that you can accomplish what is set before you.

**Through Christ, all things are possible.**

## *Lesson 20 Review and Questions*

What is the significance of the verse found in Luke chapter 22?

When have you been asked to do something you didn't want to do, even though you knew it was the right thing?  How did you feel after finishing?

Why do you think Christ prayed that God would "take this cup from him?"

What happens when we step out of our comfort zone and rely upon God to help us complete something?

What is your mission?  What are you accomplishing for God's kingdom?

What can you do to help others know Jesus as their personal savior?

Prayer used after discussion:
Dear heavenly Father, I/we thank you for sending your son so that we may have eternal life.  We pray you would anoint us the strength and wisdom to do your work, so others may know

you as their personal savior.  Help us to grow in the struggles of our daily life, knowing you are watching over us.  Amen.

## *Lesson 21 – I Am the True Vine*

### John 15: 1-2

"I am the true vine, and My Father is the vine-dresser. Every branch in Me that does not bear fruit He takes away; and every branch that bears fruit He prunes, that it may bear more fruit."

### Versus 5-7

"I am the vine, you are the branches. He who abides in Me, and I in him, bears much fruit; for without Me you can do nothing. If anyone does not abide in Me, he is cast out as a branch and is withered; and they gather them and throw them into the fire, and they are burned. If you abide in Me, and My words abide in you, you will ask what you desire, and it shall be done for you."

### Context

These two versus are describing our relationship with Christ, and "bearing fruit" or doing God's will. He is describing those people who do God's will in their lives, and are therefore "pruned" to do further work for God's kingdom. It is the Great Commission – every Christian shall bear witness of the kingdom and the salvation only offered through accepting Christ as his or her personal savior.

## What does this mean?

A leaf can't grow without a branch, tree, and roots planted firmly in the ground. A leaf grows only after a tree or plant has taken root, and grown to a point where it can flourish. These versus are describing that we cannot survive without Christ, the vine of our life. As we flourish and do God's will, God, the vine-dresser, "prunes" or replenishes us, making us ready to do more for His kingdom.

Similarly, a black belt in martial arts didn't become a black belt over night. It takes years of training, "pruning" or preparing, learning movements, understanding the discipline and self-control, and being coached by teachers/instructors who allow you to progress to new ranks.

**Allow Christ to be the vine in your life – who allows you to grow and reach new heights.**

## *Lesson 21 Review and Questions*

What does it mean to "bear fruit" as the verses describe?

Why is it important to continually bear fruit as Christians?

What is the circumstance for not bearing fruit, and why is it so important to understand?

As Christian martial artists, how can you bear fruit to fellow students, teachers, colleagues, etc?

Illustrate how your "pruning" in the study of martial arts has made you a better person?

How does God's "pruning" prepare us for greater experiences?

What occurs when we bear fruit for Christ, and focus on His will each day?

What is the Great Commission? Why should every Christian concern him/herself with this command?

Prayer used after discussion:

Dear heavenly Father, I/we give you thanks for the blessings you have given us. We ask that you would help us focus on carrying out your will. As Christ said in the garden, let thy will be done, not my own. Father, help us to give back to others what has first been given us, so that others may come to know you. Amen.

## Lesson 22 – There Are a Variety of Gifts

### I Corinthians 12: 4-11

"There are a variety of gifts, but the same Holy Spirit. There are differences of ministries, but the same Lord. And there are diversities of activities, but it is the same God who works all in all. But the gifts of the Spirit is given to each one for the profit of all: one is given the word of wisdom, another knowledge, another faith, another healing, another prophecy, another discerning of spirits....But one and the same Spirit works all these things, distributing to each one individually as He wills."

### Context

These versus are talking about the huge array of spiritual gifts given to people. Many seem very simple, but put in the context of using these gifts to glorify God, they take a new meaning for a Christian life – they are used to glorify God and other believers, not just one self. Some may appear more glamorous than others, but His gifts are provided to do His work, not for our own individual purposes.

### What does this mean?

By now, many of you are becoming aware of what you can and can't do. As an example, there's not many people who have the "smarts" of Albert Einstein, though many people use his concepts and teachings to help others in today's world. It was his initial mathematics and perceptions which have allowed the world to make great leaps forward in science and space exploration.

Similarly, you're probably becoming more familiar with at understanding what skills / movements are easier for you than for your fellow classmates. Maybe you are very flexible, maybe you have more power in your kicks and punches, or maybe you can concentrate and focus on the task at hand more so than others in the class.

Regardless of what gifts you are given – whether spiritual or physical, we need to use them to help others. Although martial arts can be considered an "individual" activity – where you learn and progress dependent on your own abilities – a martial artist often becomes his or her best when others help them with the gifts they have been given.

**Learn to understand what gifts you have been given, and use them to help others.**

## *Lesson 22 Review and Questions*

Why is it important that each person be given a unique combination of spiritual gifts?

What gifts have you been given? How have these gifts helped you or other people?

Why is it important to use the gifts God has given you? How does it benefit others?

How have you used your gifts to overcome obstacles in your life?

Name an experience in your life where someone else helped you, by using their spiritual gifts?

How have your instructors or fellow students helped you to overcome obstacles in your training?

Prayer used after discussion:
Dear heavenly Father, I/we thank you for the spiritual gifts you have given us. We ask that you would continue to hone our talents and skills so we may bless others. Father, we pray you would open our hearts to receive from others, that we may

become better people through understanding your multitude of gifts. Amen.

## *Lesson 23 – Put On Tender Mercies*

## Colossians 3:12 – 17

"Therefore, as the elect of God, holy and beloved, put on tender mercies, kindness, humility, meekness, longsuffering; bearing with one another, and forgiving one another; if anyone has a complaint against another; even as Christ forgave you, so you also must do. But above all these things put on love, which is the bond of perfection. And let the peace of God rule in your hearts, to which also you were called in one body; and be thankful. Let the word of Christ dwell in you richly in all wisdom, teaching and admonishing one another in psalms and hymns and spiritual songs...and whatever you do in word or deed, do all in the name of the Lord Jesus, giving thanks to God the Father through Him.

## Colossians 3: 22b – 24

"... obey in all things, not with eye service, as men-pleasers, but in sincerity of heart, fearing God. And whatever you do, do it with your whole heart, as to the Lord and not to men, knowing that from the Lord you will receive the reward of the inheritance; for in all things you serve the Lord."

## What does this mean

Have you ever experienced the ramifications of a bad decision? You decided to do something, and later regretted it for one or many reasons? We've all had it happen – we decide to take (or not) take action, say something to someone, or know in our gut it was a bad decision and later wish we could do it over again. We want to take "back" the consequences.

A few years ago a popular wrist band was worn by many people. The acronym, "WWJD", or "What would Jesus do..." was written on this band. It's a good reminder when we're feeling pressured to do something, or make a decision about something we're not completely comfortable.

Back in the early 1990's, my instructor had a student who wanted to spar everyone and show he was the best in class. You could say he was "crazed" with seeing if offensive martial arts really worked. While sparring with my instructor, this student decided to forget all rules of sparring, and decided to try and knock him out. Needless to say, my instructor wanted a peaceful outcome to this session, and ended it swiftly with a roundhouse kick to the back. It landed so hard the student later thought he had been kicked in the ribs! The imprint of my instructor's foot was on the student's back for the better part of a week!

I share this story because it shows what can happen when a bad decision is made. Fortunately, no one was seriously hurt. The student found out the hard way that techniques can absolutely incapacitate a person. Although my instructor may not have realized it at the time, he did "put on the tender mercies of kindness and humility." He chose not to hurt the student, but teach him a lesson before anyone got seriously hurt.

**Do things deliberately, and find peace in knowing there is order, not chaos, in the decisions made through God's will.**

## *Lesson 23 Review and Questions*

Why is it important that we forgive one another?

What does it mean to "admonish one another in psalms and hymns and spiritual songs?"

What is the difference between doing things "with eye service and men-pleasers" and with "sincerity of heart?"

Is it possible to make bad decisions when we are in God's will?

How does the discipline obtained through martial arts training allow for success?

Think of your training in the martial arts. When did you make a bad decision and what were the ramifications of that decision?

What is the significance of the story above, with the student wanting to fight no-holds-barred with the instructor?

How can this story relate to you as a Christian?

Prayer used after discussion:

Dear heavenly Father, I/we thank you for first loving us. Thank you for your grace, and undeserving love. Father, we ask you to help us do things with sincerity of heart and to know we do all things to glorify you. Help us to think of what Christ would do in times of difficulty. We pray you would grow our understanding and develop peace in our hearts. Amen

## Lesson 24 – God Reveals His Plan

### Exodus 3: 1

In Exodus, God reveals His plan for His people to be free from the Pharaoh of Egypt. God called Moses to lead His people to the Promised Land. **Verse 10**: "Then Moses said to the Lord, 'O my Lord, I am not eloquent, neither before nor since You have spoken to Your servant; but I am slow of speech and slow of tongue." The Lord said to him, "Who has made mans' mouth? Or who makes the mute, the deaf, the seeing, or the blind? Have not I, the Lord? Now therefore, go, and I will be with your mouth and teach you what you shall say..."

### Context

Chapter 3 of Exodus indicates Moses' unwillingness to answer God's calling. God called Moses through a burning bush, and yet Moses didn't want to follow God's will. Moses is concerned about how he will speak to pharaoh, what the people will say, and if they can trust Moses is doing the will of God. His mind was full of concern about *his* ability...

### What does this mean for us

How often are you asked to do something – either speak in front of people, give a presentation, or do something you felt you simply could not do. There have been times in all our lives we question, "Why me?" "Isn't there someone better suited for this calling?" What would have happened if Christ decided one day that he couldn't follow through with His "mission?"

In today's world, God obviously doesn't speak to His people through burning bushes, or through brilliant-blinding lights. I believe God's call can be subtle. We need to take time to hear what God is saying. It may be leading a class like this some day, or it may be writing a book. The important thing to remember is that we need to be open to God's call, and when He does call us, as we see in Exodus, He expects us to "pick up our cross and follow Him."

**Next time you are confronted with something challenging, or something you think you're not right for, allow God to give you the strength to carry you through.**

## *Lesson 24 Review and Questions*

Why did God call Moses to lead His people out of Egypt?

What is significant about Moses and his unwillingness to initially do God's will?

Discuss a time in your life you were asked to do something in which you said or felt, "why me?"

Why is it important to rely upon God in order to overcome these obstacles?

As a martial artist, you are often confronted with difficult, often adverse classes and testing requirements. How can you relate the story above to your martial arts training?

Discuss a time in your martial arts training where you felt similar to Moses, who felt he didn't have the capabilities or skill set to accomplish what God had called him to do.

Prayer used after discussion:
Dear heavenly Father, I/we thank you for the peace which passes all understanding. For allowing us to live in a country we can practice and speak our faith freely without risk of

persecution. Lord, we ask you to help us to overcome those trying situations in our lives. Allow us to realize you often call people out of their comfort zone in order to grow stronger in their faith. May we grow ever closer to you. Amen.

## *Lesson 25 – Peter the Disciple*

### Matthew 14: 22-33

In the 4 Gospels, we learn of Christ's life and teachings. In Matthew, we learn of Jesus walking on water. Verse 25, "Now in the fourth watch of the night Jesus went to them, walking on the sea. And when the disciples saw Him walking, they were troubled, saying "It is a ghost!" And they cried out for fear. But immediately Jesus spoke to them, saying, 'Be of good cheer! It is I; do not be afraid.' And **Peter** answered Him and said, 'Lord, if it is You, command me to come to You on the water.' When Peter had come down out of the boat, he walked on the water to go to Jesus. When he saw that the wind was loud, he was afraid; and beginning to sink he cried out, saying, 'Lord, save me!' Jesus immediately stretched out His hand and caught him... *'O you of little faith, why did you doubt?'* And when they returned to the boat the wind ceased..."

**In Matthew 26**, we learn of Jesus' Prediction of Peter's Denial. Peter states in verse 33, "Even if all are made to stumble because of You, I will never be made to stumble." Of course, we know Peter denies Christ three times when asked by the guards if he knows Jesus.

**In John 21,** Jesus speaks with Peter. Verse 15, "Jesus said to Peter, 'Simon, do you love Me more than these?' He said to Jesus, 'Yes, Lord; You know that I love You.' Jesus said to him, '**Feed My lambs**.' Jesus said to him again a second time, 'Simon, son of Jonah, do you love Me?' 'Yes Lord; You know that I love You.' Jesus said to him, '**Tend My sheep**.' He said to Peter a third time, 'Simon, son of Jonah, do you love Me?' Peter responded, 'Lord, you know all things; You know that I love You.' Jesus said to Him, '**Feed My sheep**."

From these examples, and the many others found regarding Peter, I consider the Gospels to be the story of a Christian walk – indicated by Peter's growing faith. From the versus above, we see Peter questions Jesus, then has hopeful optimism about being a part of something (walking on water), then denying Christ because of concern for himself, and eventually being called to tend and feed Christ's flock, or believers.

In similar fashion, I like to consider Peter's walk similar to a martial artist's journey. We need to keep our eye on the goal. As white belts, students question everything. As skills increase optimism and courage grow. Eventually a martial artist must deny him/herself in order to become all he/she can become.

The Gospel's are Christ's life on Earth. Martial arts training, like Peter's life, is a series of ups and downs. It's the journey of becoming, not the end result, that matters.

## *Lesson 25 Review and Questions*

How is Peter's questioning, denying, and eventual acceptance of Christ similar to our walk as Christians?

What is significant about the works, "feed my lambs...tend my sheep...feed my sheep?"

Why did Peter begin to sink while walking on the water? How does this relate to our walk with Christ?

What is the significance of these words as they relate to the Great Commission?

What is your goal as a Christian?

What is your goal as a martial artist?

Prayer used after discussion:
Dear heavenly Father, I/we thank you for your enduring patience and understanding. Father, we ask you to focus our lives on you. Help us remove all doubt and questioning, and allow us to feel enriched by your strength and guidance in our lives. May we find the hopeful optimism that only your truth can bring. Amen.

## *Lesson 26 – Christ Is Meek*

### II Corinthians 10:1

Paul is discussing humility and meekness, and says, "Christ is meek."

### Matthew 5:5

"The meek shall inherit the earth."

### Context

Meekness is generally thought of as being weak, feeble, or not being able to defend oneself. In reality, meekness takes great strength. Meekness is humility and gentleness with power. A weak person is incapable of true meekness. Christ was meek yet He had absolute power. He also exercised ultimate control since He could have called upon a legion of angels at any time (Matthew 26:52).

The meek shall inherit the earth because they have the strength of character to exercise their power with wisdom, restraint and gentleness. It does not mean those who are weak, or less fortunate shall inherit the earth simply due to a particular misfortune.

## How does this relate to me in this class

Being involved in this class and learning self-defense and martial arts is a huge responsibility! Our hope as instructors is that you walk out of this training hall and have meekness – in what you say, and what you do.

Centuries ago, students didn't pay money to learn martial arts. Students were chosen by the master instructor for their character – the ability to show meekness and humbleness (think of all the bowing in martial arts movies and eyes looking at the ground). Of course, they were also chosen for their ability to carry on the martial arts techniques and traditions.

In my class, the instructors only teach the students what they need to know at a certain belt. We want them to build their character – find patience in themselves and wait to learn that jump reverse hook kick, or the tornado kick that other's are now able to do, or the joint locks and throws that are coming in future classes. By teaching only what they need to know, we ensure they practice what is taught, vs. practicing techniques incorrectly, or wasting their energy on things they don't need to know. (Think about lesson # 19 with the student at the grunge concert).

By the time you reach black belt rank, you not only will have the skill associated with the rank, but you will have gained something much more important — similar to the schools centuries ago — the meekness of your power will lie within you, but as Christ is our example, your strength will come with restraint and gentleness and showing the Fruit of the Spirit.

**Focus on today's task, on today's teachings, and when you come to the end of your journey, you will be a more complete person — in martial arts and in character.**

## *Lesson 26 Review and Questions*

What is meekness?

Give an example of meekness?

Why do so many people consider meekness the inability to defend oneself or be physically weak?

How can you as Christian martial artists show meekness in class, with colleagues, or at home?

How can meekness make you a better person, or a better martial artist?

How can you show meekness and be a servant leader?

Prayer used after discussion:
Dear heavenly Father, I/we thank you for the example set before us in Christ Jesus. We ask you to help us seek your face, and be humble in our walk with you. Let us be servant leaders in our communities, our jobs, our schools, and our families. Help us exemplify your character, and remember Christ as our example of true meekness. Amen.

## *Lesson 27 – The Map*

### Where's the Map

A few weeks ago I traveled back to the Midwest to visit my parents. They are in the process of building a cabin some one hundred miles north of Green Bay, WI. During the winter, it gets very cold! During this recent trip my father was explaining the car was equipped with the On Star™ feature. This is a terrific feature! It's basically a hands-free phone in your car.

Being intrigued by this system and how it worked, I hit the button and an On Star representative called out, "Hello Mr. Stieg, how may we help you?" My first thought, "cool!" My dad explained that a satellite in space tracks each car with the On Star feature. Thus, when you get lost or need directions, want reservations at the last minute at your favorite restaurant, On Star is there to guide and help you!

My dad went on to explain On Star is much more than just a hands-free phone. "Traveling up north to the cabin can be dangerous. We never know if a deer may jump out in front of the car and cause an accident! On Star is almost like a guardian angel. If the car is traveling at 60 mph and immediately comes to a stop, they will call the car to determine if something occurred!  They actually know if the airbags have been deployed!  How's that for technology!"

## What does this mean

In life, as in martial arts, you need to have a "map" of where you are and where you are headed.  What's your map?  How do you decide where you are headed?  Is it random thought, or do you have a plan where you want to go?  What do you want to do in life that must take planning?

I like to think the On Star feature is similar to our Father in heaven.  I can't see either, but I know they are there.  In a moments notice, our Father in heaven is there for us.  Of course we can't hit a button and instantaneously hear His voice. He should be the creator and focus of our individual map.

In martial arts, you need to have a map of where you are headed.  Does the direction you're currently traveling get you to your destination?  If not, you want to hit the On Star button, or better yet call on God to help steer you back on course.  Throughout my training, I like to use the equation e=mc2 to understand if I'm going in the appropriate direction.  Yes, I'm borrowing this equation from Einstein's theory of relativity, but I don't mean energy, mass, or squaring the speed of light.  I know I'm headed in the right direction when my effort = mastering curriculum & character.

Outside of the training hall, I use the same "litmus test;" does my effort = mastering circumstances and character.

If you're headed in the wrong direction, pray to our heavenly Father. Ask him to steer you back on course. Use the e=mc2 equation in a way that helps drive you toward your destination. If you keep God first, seek His face, and allow His will for your life, you'll always be headed in the right direction.

**Effort = mastering character & circumstances. e=mc2. Let God be the On Star in your life, steering you in the direction you should go.**

## *Lesson 27 Review and Questions*

What is the map of your life? What are you trying to accomplish now?

Have you allowed God to create or mold your map?

How is On Star similar to a guardian angel?

What is your map or direction in martial arts?

How do you know if you're headed in the right direction?

How do you get back on track?

**Prayer used after discussion:**

Dear heavenly Father, I/we thank you for the guidance you bring to our lives. We pray you would help keep us on the path you have set out for us. Allow us to understand you are there to steer us back on track when we get lost. May we always seek your will for our lives. Amen.

## *Lesson 28 – He Equips the Called*

**God doesn't call the equipped, He equips the called...**

Wishing to encourage her young son's progress on the piano, a mother took her boy to a Paderewski concert. After they were seated, the mother spotted an old friend in the audience and walked down the aisle to greet her.

Seizing the opportunity to explore the wonders of the concert hall, the little boy rose and eventually made his way through a door marked "No Admittance."

When the house lights dimmed and the concert was about to begin, the mother returned to her seat and discovered the child was missing.

Suddenly, the curtains parted and spotlights focused on the impressive Steinway on stage. In horror, the mother saw her little boy was sitting at the keyboard, innocently picking out "Twinkle, Twinkle Little Star."

At that moment, the great piano master made his entrance, quickly moved to the piano, and whispered in the boy's ear, "Don't quit! Keep playing."

Then leaning over, the great master reached down with his left hand and began filling in the gaps. Soon his right arm reached around to the other side of the child and he added a running obligato.

Together, the old master and the young novice transformed a frightening situation into a wonderfully creative experience.

That's the way it is with God. What we can accomplish on our own is hardly noteworthy. We try our best, but the results aren't exactly graceful flowing music. But with the hand of the master, our life's work truly can be beautiful.

Next time you set out to accomplish great feats, listen carefully. You can hear the voice of the Master, whispering in your ear, "Don't quit! Keep playing." Feel His loving arms around you. Your attempts can be turned into wonderful masterpieces.

**God doesn't call the equipped, He equips the called....**

## *Lesson 28 Review and Questions*

Name an experience in your life where having God's master touch made the experience memorable.

Why is it important to allow God to work in our lives in order for us to fully comprehend His vision for our lives?

How has God equipped you to do His will?

In what way is your martial arts training similar to the young child playing the piano with the help of the master?

Share an experience in your life where you feel you have been equipped to do God's will.

Prayer used after discussion:
Dear heavenly Father, I/we thank you for your master's touch in all we accomplish. Father, we ask you to bless the actions of our day, and allow us to do your will without being afraid, or concerned how others will perceive our focus on your will. May you guide us each step, that we may create a lasting impression of your love on other's lives. Amen.

# ~ **About the Author** ~

Mr. Stieg began his training in martial arts in 1984 after seeing the movie "Karate Kid." Being from the Midwest, he found that traditional Korean and Japanese martial arts abound. Initially starting his training in traditional Tae Kwon Do (way of the hand and foot) and Hapkido (way of coordinated power), the author eventually focused his training on the latter.

After obtaining his first degree black belts in both arts in 1992, the author graduated from college and moved to California. While in Los Angeles, the author continued his study of Hapkido while training at the Kali Academy in Whittier, CA. In 1994, the author received his second degree black belt in traditional Hakpido while studying at Cho's World Hapkido Federation Black Belt Academy. Realizing cross-training was needed to become a proficient martial artist, the author combining his study of Jeet Kune Do (way of the intercepting fist) and traditional kicking and throwing arts with Muy Thai kickboxing and Wing Chun kung fu in 1998.

Most recently, the author received his third degree black belt from the World Hapkido Federation (License #5908254) in

March, 2003. Today, he teaches a combination of the arts mentioned above to students throughout Northern California.

In April of 2003, the author began teaching Christian based martial arts using the lessons found throughout this book. Realizing traditional martial arts instruction leaves much to the imagination, the author developed this book to help martial artists realize how closely knit the Fruit of the Spirit (love, joy, peace, patience, kindness, goodness, faithfulness, gentleness, and self control) is related to one's personal goals and training in the arts.

hkd_instructor@hotmail.com and visit http://www.betheldojang.org for videos and testing materials